SOS

SOS

AURORA WINTERS

CONTENTS

CHAPTER 1

Introduction to Emergency Signals

An emergency signal is a method of establishing one's presence in an emergency situation before police or fire rescuers arrive. Emergency signals are sent in cases of danger such as fires, severe weather such as tornadoes or hurricanes, or serious trauma onboard a moving vehicle. Their purpose is to draw the attention of potential rescuers and others, such as passing ships. Local cave rescue teams often suggest burning things such as rubber, insulation scraps, and wood pallets to create extra black smoke during an above-ground search. Fires may also be used to reduce bailing required when a boat is used, which aids boaters who may otherwise be too afraid to pick up a floundering swimmer to affect rescue. Emergency signals can be used by persons in distress to be rescued or helped more quickly. Distress signals are usually communicated via a visual or aural medium. These use some of the methods listed below:

• Mountain distress signals - such as the International mountain distress signal • Aircraft emergency beacon signals - such as the emergency locator transmitter • The "SOS" Morse code signal, sometimes called "letters and lights" • Code flags as emergency signals • Signaling at sea - such as flags, arms and light signals. • A "Mayday" voice signal in the voice procedure • Model rocket and high powered rocketry clubs often use high-power rockets to launch signals such as smoke, flares, or small, high powered parachutes to spot rocket drift, on a commercial range when a rocket is lost or during periods of inefficiency • Police emergency lights and sirens can also be used to attract attention.

Definition and Purpose

Emergency signals, also known as calls for distress or help, are transmitted by any means available to attract attention for the purpose of obtaining assistance. While many natural and technological emergencies rely on signals from the victim to community responders, search and rescue presents a special case due to the fact that communications may be conducted directly with the individual or be ephemerally visible as in the case of footprints in snow. The distinction is less significant with "urban searches", which search for an individual within a populated locale, as there is an excess of "rescuers" who can be called. It is safe to assume that all lost individuals in natural areas as well as in urban situations wish to make their presence known to searchers. This may be to request assistance or for notification that the searcher has located them, however, it is reasonable to assume that an individual missing for a substantial period of time has a severe condition or injury which caused him/her to become missing in the first place. To be most effective, an emergency signal must gain the attention of competent responders who can either assist directly or initiate a response from additional resources.

An emergency signal has a twofold function. Firstly, the signal must convey a distress message to those who can initiate or render assistance. This will generally consist of response agencies, but also includes relatives, friends, and ordinary civilians. Secondly, the signal must gain the attention of those authorized to assist, and commercial illumination of a company logo will not achieve this as it will serve no objective purpose. An emergency signal can be divided into two distinct signals: visual signals and audible signals. Both visual and audible signals have practical advantages and disadvantages, and in a situation where both types are being used, the victim is likely to be better off. The principle behind this is that if the victim does not get noticed by one signal type, he/she may attract attention with the other.

Types of Emergency Signals

Emergencies occurring across the seas, land, and air have led to the creation of varied forms of distress signals. There are many ways to indicate an immediately dangerous situation or a crisis. Distress can be reported by sound (screaming, yelling, or sound-producing devices), by sight (flashing lights, signal mirrors, flags and sema-phore, colored fireworks to free recoverable surface), by SDR (RID-DOR, 1995), text (e.g., sending text messages during COVID-19 restrictions), or by sending an emergency alert through different de-vices (such as the telephone carried by people on the streets, in cars, or similar uses). En route operation, mentioned that one can use a whistle and using international distress signals (e.g., flares) for signal-ing method.

Auditory signals have consistently been a viable option in a rural area, especially in wilderness and forest-bordering areas where the nearest help could possibly come from another hiker in the vicinity or from a rescue worker in the early stage. If anyone is deep within a water body, it is possible to use a whistle or comparable devices to produce a sound that could traverse the sound-reflecting surface and alert the rescuers in inland waters or shore. The audio signal is a very effective way of signaling for people in close contact with the urgent team or near an urgent service station. also stated that there are certain barriers to using audio signals in a strong wind, in snow and thick fog, or against competing EM noise over a long distance. If someone cannot make his/her voice heard above the general EM noise, the remaining options are a whistle or to use a cell-phone (if, of course, they work in mountainous or remote areas). Some of the affected women who were victims of domestic violence signaled their distress through EM ways such as tapping or using a predefined ringtone.

CHAPTER 2

The Origin of SOS

SOS: The history of an internationally recognized distress signal The signal SOS acquired international acceptance as a distress signal despite the realities that, when it originally appeared in the early 20th century, primarily on land in Western Europe and had been granted official status. This might conjure up images of mariners desperate to hold off a watery end, but its arrival on the airmanship is telling of its historical process. It was in a 1905 radiotelegraphy filing agreement between the United States, Germany, and Belgium that it declared Morse code as the preferred means of communication, which two years later included the transmitter and receiver of telegraphic messages between sparkgap transceivers and power of at least 500 watts. Morse code, and its derivatives, was also used in other technologies that relied on a regular electrical signal.

The most important thing to note about Morse's arrival was that it anticipated regulation from many communication companies. The US Navy had used telegraphic apparatus in the 1840s and during the American Civil War, and it was an immensely important development to have the wire telegraph operated by dots and dashes alone. After Morse code, the move to radio had begun, and this slower version of telex was soon developed. The Anglican Church, notably in the countries of Britain, rented out their church spires to wireless companies as early as the turn of the century. The wireless eventually became small enough to fit on an airship, and from there it began to gravitate towards seacraft. At first, most larger vessels and some smaller ones still also carried telegraphic equipment to stay in touch with land, but what a distress signal 'signing off' over a telegraphic system back then!

Development of Morse Code

Before the invention of Morse code, communication was limited by the rate at which messengers could travel. Morse code allowed electricity to be used in communication for the first time, which greatly outpaced humans and laid the foundation for many of the communication advances to come. Morse code is also fully written in longhand, so it became the first standardized transcription for telegraph communication or visual means of communication, i.e. light signals using "lighting operators." The Civil Aviation Organization dictated SOS, signaled '...—,' using its Morse code equivalents. The commercialization of radios brought with it even further standardization, both of signal types and the calls associated with each. This new system of signals and languages had the downside of making it obvious if a ship was trying to disguise itself by changing its name, but a few years passed and it became clear that new standards were needed to further organize telegraphs and reduce note-taking mistakes and sending time for basic communication. Thus, alpha telegrams were introduced, with a two-word sentence and a cut. On July 1, 1884, the time in each time zone was standardized!

A system of international code broke up when France, Norway, and Germany couldn't agree on the code and Morse code (with a few internationalized commands and no longer using quite a few signals). The United States went with the proposed 15-minute time zone shift. In the naming of Morse code, "Where are we?" a code. It was proposed in 1904 to make up a new international code. In April of 1905, the International Radiotelegraphic Convention is signed, specifying that the international distress signal should be "S O S" in Morse code for "S" (three short signals) and O (three long signals).

CHAPTER 3

Historical Uses of SOS

There are times where a call for immediate help is required, and every second counts. Throughout modern history, an international SOS signal has been used as a Morse code distress call that used to call for help over long distances. It is interesting to look back at some notable instances of when SOS was employed in times of need. The use of SOS as a distress call is often associated with the term "Save Our Souls," and the distress call is usually repeated three times in succession to ensure that it is heard and understood. In times of stress and danger, such as shipboard emergencies, Morse Code letters - specifically three short, three long, and three short or "··· — — — ···" in Morse – could be tapped out to save the crew and passengers. Its almost-urgent sense of calling resulted in the popular phrase "SOS" meaning "the international Morse code distress signal."

Though there are accounts of it possibly being earlier, the first reported use of SOS used as a distress signal was during the SS Arapahoe wreck in 1909. In a panic, James Cullen transmitted the first distress call using "SOS." The first internationally recognized use of "SOS" was on April 14, 1912, when the Titanic lookouts spotted an iceberg and tried to send an emergency signal to approaching ships. Though there is a misconception that the RMS Titanic sunk with the Morse "SOS" call, the Titanic sent the SOS distress call and CQD voice distress call as the ship was screaming for help with the German Steamship SS Frankfurt. The RMS Titanic then used the Merlin box for wireless equipment to signal that the ship was sinking 600 miles off the Grand Banks of Newfoundland.

Titanic Disaster

The sinking of the Titanic is one of the most iconic events in maritime history. Titanic, at that time, could be considered a technological marvel of architecture and aesthetics. The tragedy also has significance in emergency procedures. The ship sank after hitting an iceberg in a not-so-remote segment of the New World. Over 2200 passengers and crew were on board the ship and a call for help went from ship to ship and from the ship to the land. The call is said to be from J.P. Morgan, then a well-known wealthy figure in the United States but he was not actually present there and the actual call was made from the assault squad that was establishing wireless communications from the ship to land. The significance of the distress call made was the call sign given to it. The call sign given was not in Morse code nor the international signal for distress but a combination of the two, it was 'SOS'. The renowned 1912 invention of Morse code or The International Radiotelegraphic Convention of 1912 provided detailed description radiotelegraphic signals for regular communications and signals of distress. Although the call sign was in two letters in English and not in Morse code, the call sign was still valid which is agreement of both the previously available signaling systems.

On 14th April 1912, 'SOS', our standard signal of distress, saved human lives – The Economist, 1927. Various maritime communication and distress signaling devices were on board the Titanic when the ship sailed but only two were available when the call for help was initiated with 'SOS'. The operators present could easily get the signal through the mixed position of commercial correspondence and distress call with the equipment available for electronic telegraphic communication allowing the 'SOS' to reach other ships and also an army weather station named of Fort Worth. The distress call typed was "CQD", which was the distress call given in the Revised 1904 Marconi Radio Code, and was implored by the then British Government. The revised message, "COME QUICK – DANGER", slowly started changing letters from 'C' becoming a 'S', 'Q' to 'O' and 'D' to 'S' with the distant communication relayed by the weather stations. The second interrelated device that was being continuously tapped was the naval and marine standard warning signal being "HELP". This signal was advanced by the Titanic to the Calatif Fort while typing the "SOS" message by a man named John Phillips. Despite this, the British government still employed the "CQD". After the British government employed the signal in the vicinity and predominantly near to the site of disaster, one man boat was launched. 75 people launched the small lifeboat which could carry 65 people and a distress call was sent. The man was Harold Bride, the wireless officer.

The complete load of distress traffic in the relative close vicinity when a disaster occurred was taken by the RMS Carpathia. She was over 60 miles away from the sunken Titanic with a rate of 20 miles an hour to the northeast when the man happened to notice the call between the two wireless men. The communication was unanimously misunderstood to be the White Star Line ship Olympic, hardly 500 miles ahead of them, and the Carpathia turned changing its compass to 2580 with an exact position of 24.30 Degrees North and 30.24 Degrees West from the sun at 20.47 ST. A radio compass at land made triangulation measurements of the relative positions to arrange and marked on the chart. They did not, however, inform the approximate location to the world and neither did they made weekly distress call which is a standard in any sea disaster situation. Above ideas and distress signaling situation explain scarcely, the problem and issues that the maritime industry was facing before the implied results of these constraints. Regulatory and communication unclarity were being faced in the domain of maritime emergencies. How could a mere status signal serve enough to describe and calibrate emergencies of vector classifications, gradients of dynamic constrains, and active resource engagements in varying domains as varied as maritime environments?

CHAPTER 4

Global Adoption of SOS

As maritime trade between European navies and foreign continents grew, a universal distress signal was directionally applied. In the mid-20th century, the SOS signal was adopted as the global standard. The SOS signal was formally ratified as the international distress signal at the 1908 Berlin International Wireless Telegraph Conference. It was specified in the International Radiotelegraphic Convention that came into effect on July 1, 1908. The SOS signal gained final, official acceptance in 1912, when provisions standardizing the use of the SOS signal were placed into international law to take effect on July 1.

SOS emerged as the universal distress signal despite the use of several other earlier proposals, likely due to the widespread recognition of the signal's Morse counterpart, or three dashes, three dots, and three dashes. Empirical testing showed that personnel correctly identified local distress signals only 25% of the time. By contrast, there was nearly universal recognition of the SOS signal. For example, during a test held in New York at the time of the ratification of the international Morse code, a Daily Telegraph newsman stood in Times Square signaling into the telegraph wire. The first and most frequent word shouted out by participants: "SOS." It was at this same time that an informal meaning developed for the SOS abbreviation itself: "save our souls." The adaptation to digital communication had a tremendous impact on the character of the signal, for the very same sequence of beeps that an aural telegraph operator heard as SOS was composed of the distinct sequence of dots and dashes.

International Morse Code

It was the International Morse Code that was instrumental in the international adoption of SOS. However, Morse Code itself is no longer used and in the 1990s, it was removed from the licensing requirements, no longer being required to get an amateur radio license. All Morse Code requirements for amateur radio operation in the US were dropped in 2007. In 2001, Cospas-Sarsat stopped requiring homing beacons on 121.5 MHz. There are still some older ELTs in use that transmit on 121.5 MHz, but all new ELTs are required to transmit on 406 MHz with a digital code.

Standard operating procedures where somebody says over the radio and people come in and answer, it's all very universal. It's an internationally standard format, that's where the distress comes in as far as aviation goes. Also, if in the air, the standard emergency frequency is 121.5 MHz, so that's how we rely on somebody to hear about it and mitigate the problem. SOS is the International Morse code. Before we had stuff that was more advanced for methods of communication, SOS back in 1912-1914 was the most widely recognized system or signal that was recognized worldwide. So they decided to come up with something through the International Telegraphic Union and come up with something that would be recognized internationally as a distress...if you saw it or heard it or anything, you'd know it was an emergency. Plus, there are six people in the Long Island Coast Guard volunteers who have been operating that as one of their first means of communications.

CHAPTER 5

Evolution of Emergency Signaling Technology

The advancement in communication technology has revolutionized the way we communicate. Now, each and every second, modern individuals are kept updated with the latest news and happenings around the world. Even during emergency situations or mishaps such as terrorist attacks, calamities like cyclones, earthquakes, floods, and sundry, news now reaches a wide range of people in the soonest possible time.

In the modern day, several means are available to convey the message of distress when faced with emergency situations. People look out for visual signaling devices like the emergency lights and audio signaling devices like the sirens during these times. Adoption of technology has enabled us to immediately inform people or authorities or the services who help us to be saved or the situation implies to submit ourselves as the victims.

Visual Signaling - Visual distress signals are frequently the "last items on the list" that could save your life in an emergency; all mariners should therefore maintain a basic selection on board, as emergency communication devices can often be overpriced and are highly technical. The rising technology and greater intensity levels make flashing distress signals particularly useful for gaining attention. When a visual emergency device proves inadequate, audible signals can provide additional help, which is why air horns and other sound signals belong in all emergency kits.

Flashing signals have long been used to summon emergency responders or members of the general public. Several generations ago, an old-timer could stand on a hill and manually flash the light from a mirror to catch the attention of sailboat captains. Although a flashlight with batteries will prove to be more reliable for alerting cars, military aircraft, and personnel suffering from varying forms of disability (e.g., in a cave or snowed-in ski area).

Visual Signaling Devices

In emergency communication, visual signaling devices are often used to draw attention to a situation or signal a need for help from the public or an authority. These devices can be very simple, involving just a light or a sunscreen, or more high-tech, utilizing systems that combine visual and audible signaling. No matter how advanced the technology has become, signaling and alert methods remain useful and are typically classified in several ways: duration, characters (open and closed), sounder (automatic and fire), action (manual and automatic), technological solution adopted (engineering, electronic, or a system that is a combination of the two). Despite their differences in technology and usage, all of these systems serve a common purpose: to provide all important information about an emergency quickly and simply using one or more signals and/or devices.

But historically, human beings have not always had access to modern technology, which has forced them to use primitive methods to deal with emergencies in the past. From the time when people lived in the wilderness and had to face wild animals, fire, or other environmental adversities, cries, fire, and other visual signals were used to alert one another of the presence of danger. Naval Command (SOS) from the year 1905 became an international signal of a life-or-death situation that, on the one hand, indicates a need for immediate and major emergency assistance, that is, the search of other ships, an aeronautical service, or other rescue services, and, on the other hand, emphasizes that the ship and people on board the ship are in danger. It has practically replaced the previous international signal of danger of the "CQD", which in extraordinary cases can also be used outside the radiotelegraph service. There are three ways to visually communicate: sound, light, and false lighting. Visual signals are used in special cases in the presence of noise or poor ventilation, fire, and smoke to increase the visibility of warning or safety signals.

CHAPTER 6

Emergency Signals in Aviation

Emergency signals in aviation started in the late 1940s or early 1950s with the advent of a common emergency radio frequency band for air traffic control, known as the tower frequency of the nearest airport. When the notification of an emergency became automatic at 7600, the specific tail of a radio distress signal that was the tower frequency (also frequently blanketed the ATIS) was included in the messages given to the pilots.

There are no preserved, explicit, legally authoritative definitions in the extensive and interconnected array of authorities and operating or practice guidelines in the United States of America. The Swiss guidelines for searches at sea were an exception until 2000, giving clear signals and recommended actions in cases, along with integrating numerous sources of workable clues into the formal guidelines. These guidelines explicitly note that absent signals do not mean that vessels or aircraft are not in danger or distress. A few examples of practices in other countries are mentioned below.

The aviation industry is notable in this array of information for maintaining a somewhat formal search-and-rescue system involving explicit signals designating emergencies, and specific communication and transponder emergencies. This relatively formal written guidance is offered on two fronts: in vocabulary and communication, and in the actual physical supervision of aircraft. In addition to response guidelines, distinct routine and emergency beacon, alarm beacon, and round-robin operation signal lists are published in discussion group FAQs, in the airspace manuals, etc. These various illumination systems have particularly been given skilled attention as a matter of practical safety. Proper signals and procedural citations stand to good, absolute, and immediate paybacks: it is indeed in the sole interest of the person in distress to be rescued without any harmful delays, and of the actual rescuers to get their work done as safely and efficiently as practical.

Air Traffic Control Communication

Communication is imperative within air traffic control. Air traffic control routes landing and departing aircraft. For safety, high quality communication between pilots and air traffic controllers is urgent (also communication between two aircraft). Effective communication is beneficial in improving flying. The systems used for this form of air traffic control are VHF (very high frequency) and HF (high frequency). HF uses remote long-distance communication on the ground. The air traffic controllers generally communicate on the VHF band.

An emergency in aviation is an enigma, and when it is necessary, communication that changes it without delay is a matter of life and death. The systems are in position for this, and it is categorical. Modes A, C, S, B, and ELT (Emergency Locator Transmitter) are included in emergency communications. ELT alerts air traffic controllers on the part of an aircraft that is in an emergency circumstance and has to be entirely turned off only by ground personnel. Air traffic controllers receive a constant frequency coded broadcast in the nearby land. Maneuver electric glow systems are very poignant in the copious sky that SCP machine to set up this circumstance for urgency signal. This will alert all air traffic controllers to an emergency period. In aircraft, the transponder was added after the Second World War to assist in identifier battles (this is the I on the crap acronym - it indicates ID service with the secondary regional radar) to determine which nation a flight is in.

CHAPTER 7

Emergency Signals in Maritime

Maritime Distress Signals

An emergency is an unwanted and unfortunate situation, and it may result in loss of lives, ships, or cargo. In such circumstances, the concerned stakeholders should take prompt action to save the lives of the crew and the ship, as well as its cargo. The people who are in danger should attract the attention of others who are at a secure place. The long-range distress signal helps the survivors to attract the attention of the rescue coordination center.

Importance of Distress Signals

The use of signaling lights, flags, and sound signals to convey messages has been in use since the beginning of navigation. An effective means of signaling is equally important for the safety of shipping. The use of any signal indicating distress is forbidden except when some other means of communication cannot be employed. There are also some specific distress signals that must be used in a situation, and the other signals are not as effective in bringing rescue on time. The various distress signals in the maritime are collected in a document known as the International Code of Signals.

Historical Evolution of Distress Signals

The smoke signal is the oldest odd type of distress signal. Marco Polo is credited for introducing these during a 13th-century journey to Cathay. He wrote that the Chinese sailors activated the system by laying pieces of tinder along with lime on a bronze holder. The Hawaiian Islanders are also documented to use a comparable form of distress signal in the 19th century, by using powdered lava in iron chimneys as a means of signaling the distressed whaleships. Earlier historical records have documented their civil and military use to warn citizens of an imminent attack or to warn citizens of a national emergency.

Maritime Distress Signals

There is a brief but fascinating history behind the sound of the distress signal SOS. In the beginning, a number of different distress signals were used all across the world. The International Radiotele-graphic Conferences, held in Berlin in 1903 and 1906, sought to establish a related intergovernmental international distress signal which could be used worldwide. The regulation of the Morse Code distress signal "SOS" was first introduced in Germany in 1905 and became effective worldwide on 1 July 1908. It was, and remains to this day, the only Morse alphabet distress signal. The SOS signal has been part of the international Morse Code since 1 July 1908 and is used to attract attention in Morse. It is no longer used on radiotelegraphy frequencies, as Morse has been replaced by SITOR and NAVTEX. Despite the cessation of Morse operations, the tradi-tional distress signal SOS is still indispensable.

For navigation purposes, there is no such thing as "sailing too close to the lighthouse" during an emergency. Lighthouses do not move in rough seas or violent winds. In comparison to the many lighthouses, whether on high bluffs or low sandy shores, certain sig-nals for shipwrecked mariners, and other descriptions from past centuries which were placed here and there in places where they were difficult to find when most, if not all lights already exceeded their effective range, might have been blurred or sparks that were sent to the waves. The General Principles require that every craft engage in the maritime distress signals listed in Chapter IV of the 1988 Convention. Since these signals are instrumental to rescue craft for identifying peoples in absolute or imminent distress, appropriate use of these signals resulting in vessel choosing the best possible rescue attempt. Each signaling method is intended to be utilized only when the other approach has proven to be ineffective. When identifying an individual or a group of people in distress within the applicable distance, international conduct tries to enforce waivers to see the maritime distress information for the most likely acceptable alternative, including proper vehicles and communication methods. Rescue craft are expected to seek the place that best suits distress alerts, after receiving them.

CHAPTER 8

Emergency Signals in Land-based Scenarios

In addition to maritime and air emergencies, emergency signals can be crucial in land-based scenarios such as mountain and wilderness rescue. Terrestrial emergencies have their unique challenges. In 1964, Boyes, then editor of the British publication Search and Rescue, referred to "the great variation in beliefs and habits of people lost in remote or semi-remote areas." Modern wilderness medicine specialists agree that this statement is still accurate today. To save civilians, soldiers, scouts, hunters, and hikers in a wide range of ecosystems, emergency signals must be understood in the context of the particular environment. Cities, woods, mountains, and deserts are all very different places to become lost.

Distress signals in mountains above 15,000 feet in the Himalayas are often transmitted via permanently manned radio relay stations. On the other hand, in the American southwestern desert, due to the nature of the seemingly identical terrain, "extensive tracking operations" are required to locate a lost hiker. Most land-based emergencies occur in rural or park settings, Hawai'i being a challenge where branch and stick signals may look like "retro-scripting desert" and camouflage netting on a downed helicopter simulates the surrounding Virginia forest. Forest rangers are normally summoned through crowd-sourced "urban connectivity": locals on day-hikes, hunters, and foragers are the key reason search parties learn that a "calm and experienced hiker" is missing.

Mountain and Wilderness Rescue

The specialized domain of mountain and wilderness rescue alleviates some of the difficulties of rescue at sea but introduces new difficulties. Rather than having to gain the sight or ear of passing ships and aircraft that are often hundreds of meters long, land-based distress signaling operations rely on getting the attention of local crews on the ground and extract the victims from the site of the emergency by carrying them by land- or water-based vehicle for clearing the area so that air-based vehicles can land and take-off. Devices must also effectively signal when there may not be any rescuer nearby for thousands of kilometers. The mountain and wilderness also create specific survival challenges, such as rapidly changing weather patterns and temporary (e.g., high elevation) or long-term (e.g., under tree cover) obstructions of the satellite communication service.

Effective signals can allow the victim to become their own rescuer by calling for help and providing support to the rescue operation. Such signed calls can reduce the time-to-rescue, and thus allow a greater number of simultaneous ongoing rescue operations, which can reduce casualties and improve socio-economic development in remote and rural areas of the world, especially in low- and middle-income countries with histories of tropical cyclones. The more quickly victims can be extracted from increasingly remote locations, the higher the survivorship for a broad range of illnesses and injuries as medical care becomes inaccessible, especially in the context of climate change, increases in severe disaster events, and broad-based rural-to-urban migration.

CHAPTER 9

Cultural and Media Impact of SOS

As the de facto international Morse code distress signal, SOS has become more than a simple call on operator frequencies. Public perceptions of the call as an audio siren of distress were forged by hundreds of fictional characters who, from the early 20th century onward, called for help via SOS symbols comprising both letters and soundtracks. As befitting the distress call from the time of its adoption, SOS transmission numbers reported during 20th-century wireline distress were globally high, topping 37 times the 3 dot and 3 stripe signal of the day, during the early twentieth century telegraph distress era. This study traces the foundational professional messaging work that handed SOS to the public in order to answer a simple question: Why has SOS been shown in English in fiction as a worldwide distress symbol.

The topic reported on is the international distress signal SOS. SOS serves for dozential, not arithmetic, communications, as detailed by the parent study. It is expressed as a long sound and a long letter in printed or lit form. Throughout the illustrated 110-plus years of our inbox searches, distress-related messages have, for most parts of the period, been the most commonly reported. Campaigns like those detailed above use television, movies, comic strips, advertisements, tee-shirts, records, and buttons to attract people's attention, then follow with straight-to-the-mouth commercial or social justice seriousness. Such campaigns are mockingly skewered; they prefer to settle around neither villains nor heroes of mass media culture; and they are recorded only, if and only, in the annals of soapbox messaging.

Use in Popular Culture

Since being brought into international focus in 1905, SOS has appeared in a variety of popular media, from published works of both fiction and non-fiction, the silver screen, radio, music, and video games. As the most well-known signal of distress in Western society, its use in popular culture has been adapted into parodies and forms of satire, often being used as an emblem of distress for comedic effect. Yet it has been explored in enough media earnestly to have had a significant lingering social and cultural impact, helping form ideas of what an emergency signal is and should be.

SOS as a symbol appears most frequently in the genres of thriller, adventure, and disaster scenarios, narratively calling for a defeat of social and/or technological isolation, and as a gateway between civilization and the other.

In fewer cases, SOS has appeared in a broader range of genres, which use it as a keystone to touch on topics such as community, identity, and politics. It has been used to nudge the audience to see themselves as part of a greater collective and their isolation or individualism as a problem in and of itself. Distinctively different from beliefs about the technology and techniques of distress signaling, beliefs about appropriate mediums and the characteristics of emergency radio messages have seen semi-regular artistic depictions for over one hundred years across multiple forms of media.

SOS has been, and in parts of the world where radio is still widely used, is known as the standard internationally understood radio call or whistle for distress. SOS signals and visual depictions have also started being referred to in narratively self-referential fashion, meaning SOS within the media is often depicted alongside some form of knowledge the characters have of SOS.

CHAPTER 10

Contemporary Applications of SOS

SOS is synchronized into numerous GPS applications, like the ability to mark a location on a map or route planner indicating the point designated as "SOS" or "Help" for emergency situations. Even more advanced and sophisticated than an international Morse code signal in both its complexity and level of technology, the personal GPS-based emergency beacon sends an SOS signal via satellite to emergency request centers. The signal carries with it a unique registration number that is associated with the device's owner. Search and rescue authorities use this number to find the device registration information to best coordinate a response. At the time of registration, the owner also supplies a profile of the user's abilities, experience, and medical history. There are several kinds of emergency beacons for land, sea, and air that communicate depending on the location. They meet the needs of the Federal Communications Commission (FCC), Canada's Office of Spectrum Management (OSM), and National Oceanic and Atmospheric Administration (NOAA) specifications.

Of course, GPS is not the only technology used in sending or verifying an SOS as a standard feature in mobile phones. At least in the

United States, several distress signals have been developed to send via text message. Newer car models are being equipped with automatic SOS technology so that the car "knows" the nature and magnitude of the crash when there are serious vehicle accidents. When this happens, the vehicle for the given service will phone directly to 911, sending the precise location of the accident (when the driver does not respond to an automated call from the service, which might accompany an SOS signal activated by the vehicle's occupants). Emergency service phone operators might follow up on an SOS call by contacting the named in-case-of-emergency (ICE) numbers in the cell phone's address book. When mobile phones send an SOS, the device sometimes includes information about its location within the form of either GPS or cellular triangulation. How this is done can often help emergency responders find people faster as narrow a search area as possible so resources can be applied with efficiency.

GPS and Satellite Emergency Beacons

The last 20 years have brought many changes to the ways that people can signal for help in a remote, distressing situation. These changes have mostly sprung from the advent of widespread GPS signal reception and satellite technology. Portable satellite phones and satellite emergency beacons are the current state of the art in signals and calls for help. The family of Bendix King AeroShell emergency beacons, a collection of devices that could activate themselves in a crash and send out a radio beacon signal that passed over an international distress satellite and was picked up by an international network of geostationary satellites, was the first form of actual, physical distress signal. A series of other physical distress signals saw limited deployment and acceptance after AeroShell.

The Yarmouth County SOS save is one of the rare cases of a commercial beacon sending a signal marked with SOS actually being used for an aviation-related rescue: within hours of the save (depending on the time zone), a Joint Rescue Coordination Center in Singapore sent two business jets to pick up the crew of a crashed commercial jet in a remote Indonesian swamp. The Singapore military analyzed the signal, and the SAR mission received the data in near-real-time to decide the signal's possible veracity. Appropriate authorities and assistance were dispatched automatically, with SMS alerts received by key search-and-rescue stakeholders such as local SAR officials and district air traffic control inspectors notified of the situation and continuously appraised of the signal's location. The SOS tech-mark-point report above was produced with a generated signal after the completion of a service flight. Pop 'Save' No. 1 - 0000000223 - 24 March 2022: Cont. Vol. Digital Assets. Other signal analysts likewise received timely alerts of the distress signal.

CHAPTER 11

Legal and Regulatory Framework for Emergency Signa

Although the signal SOS seems universally communicated, different regulations exist in different countries for the transmission of a distress call. These exist in special regulations and technical systems for distress alerts: either at frequencies outside or within the bands issued or monitored by the mobile service, and in the use of the distress alert signal. A distinction is also drawn between alerting services provided primarily for survival and search and rescue, and those provided primarily for the protection of property. International law (SOSC1.8 and 8.8) prohibits the use of the word SOS and the sequence in an emergency wavelength message if it does not constitute an emergency, and it prohibits the misuse of distress signals.

Regulations also exist for the transmission of distress alerts and calls for assistance in other services. The International Telecommunication Union's radio regulations contain specific requirements about the conditions for transmitting distress alerts, urgent calls, safety communications (emergency), and calls for medical assistance in the various services, the frequencies on which these transmissions are to be made, the nature of the authorized emission, and where appropriate, that of the authorized signals. The International Mobile Telecommunications (IMT-2000) regulations of the International Telecommunication Union give a translation of the distress alert in English, French, and Spanish, and add that those signs "shall constitute the only call for help which is able to connect 112, 911, 000, and 08 to the public network, which means the distress calls, understood as the necessary communication to guarantee the arrival of immediate rescue teams, until eventually to the police, and operating independently of the network used (landline, mobile telephone, or internet) or additional services. There are international regulations and protocols that deal with the relationships of distress signals received on earth to search and rescue organizations. Enforcement is based internationally on resolutions and contracts between operators.

International Maritime Organization Regulations
The IMO was established after certain consequences of non-standardized signals endangering the lives of sailors and passengers were identified as evident challenges in the maritime communication culture. Several communication regulations governing the proscription of the use of signals other than those specified in distress, urgency or safety situations and the development of radio regulations have been included in the IMO, which are converted into regulations and applicable law in each country. These regulations apply to all ships, regardless of tonnage, type, location, and mobility. In this context, ships in flag and registered states, the owner of ships, ship operations, the captain, crew, certain radio officers, equipment and various stations are closely and strictly monitored and supervised by the LRIT supervisors, office personnel, healthcare providers, inspectors, controllers and auditors.

Within the scope of continuous inspections and terminal inspections, the devices and equipment used in e-navigation, satellite navigation and satellite tracking systems on LRIT were designed and developed in injury, down, sick, and emergency signals and are monitored and reported in detail. The International Regulations and Legislation in effect today for the exchange of vessels in danger, mobilization of search and rescue (SAR) services, sharing the status of people in danger and the area they are located are as follows.

CHAPTER 12

Psychological and Societal Implications of Emergen

More than simply the subject of aerograms, emergency signals constitute a phenomenon worth getting to know in and of themselves. Why the interest in them? They offer us one of the few hints that we have of cryptic behavior. Distress is so fundamental a phenomenon that it is far less likely to become manifest than any of the many forms of life's expression which, superficially, present themselves in normal behavior. Furthermore, distress is apparently so definitive that it constitutes a powerful propellant of behavior whenever such a signal elicits the necessary empathetic response. How these empathetic responses can be switched has been demonstrated effectively in many animal species. Distress is at the heart of social behavior in which signaling, and the response to signals, is unambiguous, hard-wired and carries limited ambiguity. It is thus very likely that such a very strongly scripted and specialized signaling system has deeper psychological roots and is interwoven with natural selection. The mechanisms of signaling and responder-style behavior are relatively late arrivals and are anticipated by time-honored psychological and social strategies, suggesting that those mechanisms probably tap into pre-existing infrastructure, albeit in highly constrained or specialized ways.

Society is bound to be typically structured in such a fashion that the manner in which signals are handled is of the greatest importance. Indeed: under one interpretation the salient signals advertise the stress itself in those sending them: the signal is not merely strange in a given population, denoting a departure from the norm, but strange in an absolute sense, poignantly advertising an emotional state of the signaller. Under such an interpretation, the costliness of expressions of distress is unlikely to be motivated in any weak sense, for fundamentally these signals are honest advertisements that greatly depress fitness. Helping is the obverse of the coin, distress advertising one side of the coin, the empathetic response the other. We would expect this to inform current theory on the ultimate aspects of signaling behavior. And so it does, but in a highly paradoxical way.

Impact on Human Behavior in Crisis Situations

Distress signals are the attempt of a person, who is in an emergency, to obtain help in an attempt to protect life. In the modern radio technology, the term for this transmission for sending is SOS. Like any other sounds, distress signals with alerting and fear-inducing properties affect human behaviour, offspring, even the muscles and visual perception. Sound processing depends on the acoustical frequencies, the intensity and the temporal interferences of the single sound as well as the interferences of multiple sounds. In the case of distress signals – with fear-inducing properties – its physical and psychological aspects influence the human experience.

A modular approach or a simple prediction of responding behaviour does not work for various reasons. The response processes including attentive capture and the motoric response towards an acoustic signal can be strongly influenced by cognitive, subjective aspects and motivation. These findings have practical implications for the design of acoustic signals and their presentational mode. Ecological valid distress communication signals, which have emergency situations' criterion validity make physiological, self-reported and behavioural responses to them likely. Communication of the need for help can, thus, reduce our distress. Ecological valid distress signals for experimentally induced situations are very likely to contain distressing vocalizations according to the review of endemic and experimentally validated signals. Emergency telephone calls provide some additional examples of communication of distress during which the pattern varies interindividually, dependent on tasks and listener experience. These findings support the urgent need to study communication of distress signals in double-tone signals for actual emergency calls.

CHAPTER 13

Future Trends in Emergency Signaling Technology

Embracing the potential of advanced technology has resulted in numerous improvements to the art and science of emergency signaling. Current and future systems designed to detect and verify signals and dispatch emergency response resources continue the trend of improvements over time. In this section, a number of recent and imminent technological developments are discussed. These advancements are divided into two categories: those for signaling, the origin of the distress notification that the user seeks to generate, and those for response, the means and media used by those providing emergency rescue to detect and respond to a user's distress.

For signaling systems, significant potential exists in the use of UAS platforms as a search platform for signal detection. The artificial vision capabilities of some such platforms have been used successfully to detect offshore survivor life rafts. Future UAS using advanced machine learning and artificial intelligence capabilities may expand the range of signals detected both during normal operations and under adverse weather conditions or the physical placement of the survivor. The user signals generated by these devices may range from visual, especially infrared as an aid to night detection, to acoustic distress signals that recent research suggests may be effective at longer ranges than visual signals when operating over flat terrain. Trisonics has patented an AUV outfitted with a mode-synchronized location tag that allows high-resolution localization of any distress signal in the communication module. An AUV mirrored the range over which earlier Soviet-developed communications from a transfer capsule reach rescue forces able to respond. The result was a dramatic reduction in AAV search and rescue resources. In American aerospace engineering, in the late 20th century, researchers retrofitted a set of ionizable signal flares to acquire an approximate position and built a high-frequency communications technology for special short-haul satellite signals for a Global Positioning System (GPS) location.

Innovations in Signal Detection and Response

Traditionally, signals and call signs have been used since ancient times to facilitate the detection of distress, communicate the need for help, and signal the response. From the primitive methods to the modern technological approaches, the evolution of signal and call sign detection—a history in the telling—suggests that the system is yet to be more technologically sound and effective by allowing for distresses that are easier to detect and, once detected, are more effectively communicated in a more timely fashion so that the response will be quicker. In essence, with the volume of data traffic on the waterways, carriers are unable to respond to every digital SOS in real time. As a result, the SOS is losing its value as an immediate distress signal.

The emergency signals of the future are likely to be detected and located via weak radio signals that are not primarily intended for distress communication. Bluetooth, Wi-Fi, Inmarsat, satellite phone, and marine Automatic Identification System (AIS) may function as signals of distress using stationary listening posts or towers. Future emergency signals may also be detected by the EOT in mobile phones at the destination as signals that are unusual for a journey. The data of these calls must be digitalized and made accessible to software that performs surveillance in real time, detecting those that are unusual and meet parameters approximating a distress.